LEVEL
3
AGES 7 AND 8

CALIFORNIA GOLD RUSH

Peter and Connie Roop

SCHOLASTIC
REFERENCE

PHOTO CREDITS:

Cover: Bettmann/Corbis; back cover: North Wind Pictures. Page 1, 3, 4: North Wind
Pictures; 6: Brown Brothers; 7: North Wind Pictures; 8: The Bancroft Library, University
of California; 9: North Wind Pictures; 10: Bettmann/Corbis; 12, 13, 14: North Wind
Pictures; 15: Culver Pictures; 17, 18, 20, 22: North Wind Pictures; 23: Tom
McHugh/California Academy of Sciences/Photo Researchers, Inc.; 25: Archive Photos; 27:
The Bancroft Library, University of California; 29: Levi Strauss & Co.; 30: Culver
Pictures; 31: Hulton/Archive; 32, 33: North Wind Pictures; 34: The Society of California
Pioneers; 36: Culver Pictures; 37: Brown Brothers; 38: Courtesy of Marshall Gold
Discovery State Historic Park, Coloma, CA; 39: North Wind Pictures; 41: Dave
Bartruff/Corbis; 43, 44: Robert Holmes/Corbis.

Library of Congress Cataloging-in-Publication Data available.

ISBN 0-439-27315-3

Book design by Kristina Albertson and Nancy Sabato
Photo research by Sarah Longacre

10 9 8 7 6 5   04 05

Printed in the U.S.A.   23

First trade printing, September 2002

We are grateful to Francie Alexander, reading specialist,
and to Adele Brodkin, Ph.D., developmental psychologist,
for their contributions to the development of this series.

The authors would like to thank John Hutchinson of the
Marshall Gold Discovery State Historic Park in Coloma, California.
John's knowledge, insights, and comments made this a better book.

• • • CONTENTS • • •

CHAPTER ONE • GOLD FEVER!   5

CHAPTER TWO • CALIFORNIA OR BUST!   11

CHAPTER THREE • STRIKING IT RICH!   21

CHAPTER FOUR • AFTER THE RUSH   35

CHRONOLOGY   45

GLOSSARY   46

INDEX   47

NOTE TO PARENTS   48

FOR FURTHER READING   48

A woodcut shows Sutter's Mill, California.

GOLD FEVER!

It was January 24, 1848. The sun rose over the California hills. James Marshall was up at dawn. He had to work on a new sawmill.

Looking into a hole in the ground by the sawmill, he saw a yellow rock. It was about the size and shape of a pea. Marshall picked up the shiny pebble and made history.

The rock was gold! James Marshall put the rock in his hat. He ran to show the other men working on the mill.

Captain John Sutter and James Marshall owned the sawmill where Marshall had been digging. Captain Sutter told Marshall to keep his discovery a secret. But, somehow, news of the gold spread quickly.

First tens, then hundreds, then thousands of people rushed to California. They all came to **strike it rich** finding gold!

James Marshall

For many years, California had been part of Mexico. By 1848, California was owned by the United States. But it was not a state. Only about 2,000 Americans lived in California at this time.

A map of California under the Mexican government

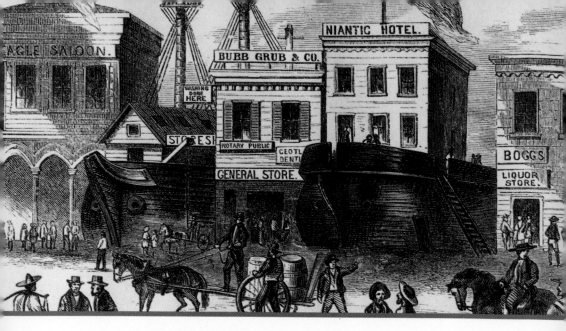

Ships abandoned in San Francisco Bay were used as hotels and stores in the early days of the gold rush.

By 1849, things had changed. People from all around the world were excited about the gold. Farmers stopped digging in their fields. They went to California to dig for gold. Teachers quit teaching. Bakers stopped baking. Sailors jumped off their ships. Shopkeepers closed their stores. Families packed and left their homes.

They all had **gold fever**!

The only cure for gold fever was to get to California. This rush of folks to find gold was the largest **gold rush** ever in the United States. The people who came in 1849 were called "forty-niners." So many people came that California became the thirty-first state on September 9, 1850. James Marshall's discovery of gold did indeed change history.

JOHN SUTTER

John Sutter moved to America from Switzerland in 1834. He came to California in 1839. Posing as an army captain (which he really wasn't), Sutter convinced the Mexican government to give him fifty thousand acres (500 hectares) of land.

In 1847, Sutter needed lumber. He decided to build a sawmill on the American River. On January 24, 1848, James Marshall discovered gold while working on that sawmill.

CALIFORNIA OR BUST!

"**O**h, Susannah, don't you cry for me. I'm going to California with a wash pan on my knee!" This was a favorite song of the forty-niners. When gold seekers left their homes, they were excited. They bragged about how rich they would be. They thought there was so much gold that they would only have to pick it up and put it in their pockets.

Artwork shows travelers struggling with the sails during a storm on their way around South America.

But just getting to the gold mines was hard. The trip was not cheap. California was far away from where most people lived.

Some people took boats all the way around South America to reach California. This was more than 15,000 miles (24,140 kilometers)! They sailed into huge storms, and sometimes ships sank. People got sick on the long voyage. A lucky ship took only six months to reach its destination. Some ships sailed for a year before reaching California!

Other forty-niners sailed to Mexico, Panama, or Nicaragua. They got off their boats, and then struggled across deserts or through jungles. Some had to paddle heavy canoes for many miles (kilometers). Bugs bit them. They got sick from drinking bad water. Many ran out of food.

Once they had crossed the land, the travelers had to wait for a ship to pick them up. The ship would carry them the rest of the way to California. Many waited for weeks or months.

Crossing Panama was not an easy way to reach California.

Gold-seekers bound for California on a sailing ship

People from China, South America, and Australia also had difficult sea voyages. They sailed across thousands of miles (kilometers) of ocean to reach California, and gold.

Many forty-niners did not want to reach the gold fields by boat. They traveled on land across America, instead. Some walked or rode horses. A man named Brookmire from Pennsylvania hiked, pushing his wheelbarrow all the way to California!

This miner has loaded his horse with everything he might need to find gold.

Most people packed their wash pans, shovels, food, guns, and clothes into covered wagons. They rolled across America. Many of these forty-niners soon found out that they had carried too much. They just threw out things like beds, books, pots, pans, and chairs along the way. One man who loved to read would pick up a book, read it, and then trade it for another discarded book. He had plenty of books to read—all the way to California!

These forty-niners in their covered wagons followed trails overland. The Oregon Trail was the best known. Another popular path was the Mormon Trail.

In this woodcut, travelers make camp on the Oregon Trail and prepare to spend the night.

This woodcut shows how hard it was to travel all the way to California by wagon.

Travel on land was just as difficult as a sea voyage. Two thousand miles (3,218 kilometers) of rivers, prairies, deserts, and mountains had to be crossed. There were strong winds and terrible storms to be weathered. Food ran out and children cried from hunger. Wagon wheels broke. The oxen pulling the wagons died. People got sick. The overland trip across America took five months or more.

No matter how they traveled, the forty-niners were eager and excited to get to California. They wanted to get rich— quick! Thousands made it. But thousands of others went **bust** trying.

COVERED WAGON LIFE

In 1849, Sarah Royce set out for California in a covered wagon. Her group had one thin guidebook. Her wagon, pulled by six oxen and two cows, frequently got stuck in mud or the wheels broke. She was often hungry and cold. When there was no wood, Sarah cooked over fires made from buffalo chips—dried buffalo dung.

Sarah rarely bathed because water was often scarce. Her skin turned dark from the wind, smoke, and sun. Some people in her group died from accidents. Others perished from sickness. In other words, Sarah "Saw the Elephant." This is the term forty-niners used to describe all the difficulties and hardships they faced in their rush for gold. Sarah made it to California, one of only two women in her mining camp, which was located near Hangtown.

STRIKING IT RICH!

The first forty-niners to reach California were lucky. Gold was fairly easy to find. Gold flakes and nuggets could be discovered in streams, rivers, or soft dirt. The miners just had to dig or pan for the gold. They used knives, shovels, bowls, and big, round pans to get gold.

Digging for gold was not too hard in the early days of the gold rush. But panning for gold often meant standing in cold water for hours swirling water and dirt in a pan.

Gold is very heavy. It sinks to the bottom of a miner's pan. Rocks and other material could be swirled out. The miner then picked out the gold and carefully saved it. Most miners kept the gold they found in leather bags.

A miner pans for gold in a woodcut of California gold rush days.

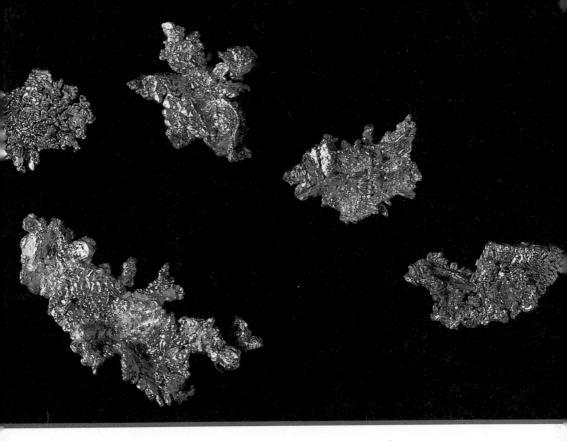

Gold nuggets come in all shapes and sizes.

Some gold looked like corn flakes. Other pieces were the size of peanuts. Lucky miners found nuggets as big as apples! And a few found chunks as large as a loaf of bread. The largest single piece of gold found during the gold rush weighed 195 pounds (74 kilograms) and was as big as a pillow!

Gold was sometimes found in strange, unexpected places. One day a woman swept the dirt floor of her cabin. When she emptied her dustpan, she had more than $500 worth of gold!

A hungry man caught a salmon and cooked it in his kettle. When he took the cooked fish out, he found the bottom of the kettle covered with gold!

One time some men were burying a friend who had died. As the minister preached, the men suddenly began scrambling in the dirt. They had spotted gold in the dirt where they had dug their friend's grave. Even the minister stopped preaching to join the hunt.

Later, when more people came, they discovered that the easy gold was gone.

Miners had to look for new places to **stake** their **claim** to dig or pan. Some used strong **jets** or streams of water from hoses to wash gold out of hills. Others blasted rocks with black gunpowder to shake loose the gold.

This illustration shows miners using jets of water to wash gold out of a California hillside.

Not many miners got rich during the gold rush. Some found only about a dollar's worth of gold each day. A few filled tin cups with 500 dollars' worth of gold a day. The lucky ones dug or panned 2,000 dollars' worth of gold in a day. Most miners found only enough to buy food and supplies.

Prices were high in California. There was little cash money, so miners paid in gold. One pound (.5 kilograms) of butter cost $6 in gold. A loaf of hard bread cost $2. A pair of shoes was $50, and a blanket sold for $100.

An 1850 advertisement offers all sorts of things miners might need for sale.

GOOD NEWS

FOR

MINERS.

NEW GOODS,

PROVISIONS, TOOLS,

CLOTHING, &c. &c.

GREAT BARGAINS!

JUST RECEIVED BY THE SUBSCRIBERS, AT THE LARGE TENT ON THE HILL,

A superior Lot of New, Valuable and most DESIRABLE GOODS for Miners and for residents also. Among them are the following:

STAPLE PROVISIONS AND STORES.

Pork, Flour, Bread, Beef, Hams, Mackerel, Sugar, Molasses, Coffee, Teas, Butter & Cheese, Pickles, Beans, Peas, Rice, Chocolate, Spices, Salt, Soap, Vinegar, &c.

EXTRA PROVISIONS AND STORES.

Every variety of Preserved Meats and Vegetables and Fruits, [more than eighty different kinds.] Tongues and Sounds; Smoked Halibut; Dry Cod Fish; Eggs fresh and fine; Figs, Raisins, Almonds and Nuts; China Preserves; China Bread and Cakes; Butter Crackers, Boston Crackers, and many other very desirable and *choice bits.*

DESIRABLE GOODS FOR COMFORT AND HEALTH.

Patent Cot Bedsteads, Mattresses and Pillows, Blankets and Comforters. Also, in Clothing—Overcoats, Jackets, Miner's heavy Velvet Coats and Pantaloons, Woolen Pants, Guernsey Frocks, Flannel Shirts and Drawers, Stockings and Socks, Boots, Shoes; Rubber Waders, Coats, Blankets, &c.

MINING TOOLS, &c.; BUILDING MATERIALS, &c.

Cradles, Shovels, Spades, Hoes, Picks, Axes, Hatchets, Hammers; every variety of Workman's Tools, Nails, Screws, Brads, &c.

SUPERIOR GOLD SCALES.　　　　MEDICINE CHESTS, &c.

Superior Medicine Chests, well assorted, together with the principal Important Medicines for Dysentery, Fever and Fever and Ague, Scurvy, &c.

N.B.—Important Express Arrangement for Miners.

The Subscribers will run an EXPRESS to and from every Steamer, carrying and returning Letters for the Post Office and Expresses to the States. Also, conveying *"GOLD DUST"* or Parcels, to and from the Mines to the Banking Houses, or the several Expresses for the States, insuring their safety.———The various *NEWSPAPERS*, from the Eastern, Western and Southern States, will also be found on sale at our stores, together with a large stock of *BOOKS* and *PAMPHLETS* constantly on hand.

Excelsior Tent, Mormon Island,
　　January 1, 1850.

ALTA CALIFORNIA PRESS.

WARREN & CO.

Many forty-niners made money selling things the miners needed. These businesspeople bought cheap food, tents, and tools. Then they sold them to the miners, charging high prices. These folks struck it rich without ever panning or mining for gold.

Levi Strauss made tents out of canvas. Then he had an idea that turned out to be more valuable than gold. He saw how quickly miners wore out their pants. So he made sturdy pants out of canvas. His strong jeans became very popular with the miners. They called Strauss's pants "Levi's." You can still buy Levis® today!

His jeans were so sturdy that Levi Strauss promised miners "A new pair free if they rip."

An illustration shows miners making themselves at home in their camp.

As more and more forty-niners arrived, mining camps became towns. Most miners lived first in tents. If they found enough gold, they bought lumber and built wooden cabins. Fire often burned down towns. Some towns burned more than once.

The miners often named their towns. Places with lots of bugs were called Bedbug or Fleatown. Tough towns were called Rough and Ready, Hangtown, Chicken Thief Flat, and Cut Throat. Others were called Gold Run, You Bet, and Last Chance. Even though they were usually tired after a hard day of looking for gold, the forty-niners still could make jokes.

The Gold Hill mining camp had a lucky name!

Sometimes there was trouble in gold rush towns. The first forty-niners met few thieves. But as more people came to California, more robbers and cheats came, too. Sometimes a miner would steal another miner's claim, or place to dig gold. This was called **claim jumping**.

Miners sometimes had to take the law into their own hands during the California gold rush.

MINING METHODS

Panning for gold in streams and rivers was the simplest mining method. Other miners used a wooden box or hollowed log called a cradle. Little boards were nailed along the bottom of the cradle. One end was left open. Dirt and  water were rocked in the cradle. The heavy gold settled behind the wooden strips. A "Long Tom" was a long, shallow wooden container open at both ends. It took three miners to fill the container with rock from the riverbed, wash it, and hopefully find gold.

Some miners, nicknamed "coyotes," dug holes and tunnels in the ground. These were called "dry diggings."

There were not many police officers or judges in California until after the gold rush days were over. So, the miners took law and order into their own hands. Claim jumpers and other lawbreakers were quickly run out of camp.

Miners sometimes brought their gold to express companies like this one.

CHAPTER FOUR

AFTER THE RUSH

James Marshall, the man who first found California gold, was called a "human good-luck charm." Miners followed him everywhere he went. They hoped he would lead them to more gold. But Marshall's luck ran out. He actually did not find much gold. He died in 1885 with little money.

By 1852, most easy-to-find gold was gone. It became harder and harder for one miner, or a team of miners, to dig enough gold to even pay for food. Soon, big companies with lots of machines began digging for gold. The miners could not keep up with the machines.

The Parks' Bar Company had lots of men and machinery on their claim, as this newspaper illustration shows.

Miners with small claims struggled to find enough gold to pay everyday expenses.

Many forty-niners gave up, left California, and headed home, broke and empty-handed.

There were some happy endings, of course. Mr. Brookmire, who had walked to California pushing a wheelbarrow, went home to Pennsylvania with fifteen thousand dollars in gold. Al Jackson and his wife, Marie, gave their tools, pots and pans, guns, and a banjo to friends. With their gold in hand, they sailed home to Connecticut.

This photo shows Sarah and Andrew Monroe (center) with their children. Andrew's mother was brought to California as a slave, but gained her freedom when California became a state in 1850. With money earned as a cook and a washerwoman, she bought Andrew and Sarah out of slavery in Missouri. Andrew Monroe became a landowner whose ranch included the gold discovery site at Sutter's Mill.

Other forty-niners stayed and became teachers, loggers, farmers, builders, and shopkeepers. Some did the same jobs they had done before they caught gold fever. Many more began new lives under the sunny California sky.

CHINESE FORTY-NINERS
Many Chinese sailed six thousand miles (9,556 kilometers) across the Pacific Ocean to reach the  "golden mountains" of California. By 1852, more than twenty thousand Chinese were mining gold or selling food, tools, and other items needed by the forty-niners. At first, when gold was plentiful, the polite, hardworking Chinese were treated well. Later, as the easy gold ran out, some white forty-niners resented the foreigners and treated the Chinese poorly. Many Chinese-Americans today are descendants of these Chinese forty-niners.

More than half a million people moved to California during the gold rush. They came from every state in the country and from seventy different nations. These forty-niners, and those who followed in their footsteps, built California.

Today, gold is still found in California's rivers and streams. Old mines are being opened again. Modern miners use special machines to hunt for gold.

But people still pan and dig for gold. They want to know what it felt like to be a forty-niner. Some of them still hope to strike it rich!

A modern-day miner pans for gold in Coloma, California.

Today, Californians honor the forty-niners who helped create their state. Each year, on January 24 (the date Marshall found gold), California celebrates Gold Discovery Day. The state motto is "**Eureka!**" This means "I have found it (gold)!"

In 1904, the beautiful golden poppy became the official California state flower. The gold rush even gave California its official nickname—the "Golden State."

This monument in Coloma's Marshall Gold Discovery State Park is dedicated to James Marshall.

A replica of Sutter's Mill is part of Marshall Gold Discovery State Park.

When James Marshall first picked up a golden pebble in 1848, he did not know what would happen. No one did. By finding gold, he started a chain of events that led to the California gold rush.

• • • CHRONOLOGY • • •

1839	John Sutter arrives in California
January 24, 1848	James Marshall discovers gold in California
1848	California added to territories of the United States after the Mexican War
1849	California gold rush begins
1850	California becomes the 31st state
1852	Last major year of the California gold rush
1854	195-pound (74-kilogram) piece of gold, the largest ever, found at Carson Hill
1865	Mark Twain visits California and writes his famous story, "The Celebrated Jumping Frog of Calaveras County"
1880	John Sutter dies
1885	James Marshall dies

bust—to run out of money; be a failure

claim—the land a miner staked as his own place to dig or pan for gold

claim jumping—stealing another miner's land

Eureka!—"I have found it!" Miners shouted this when they found gold.

gold fever—the desire to find gold

gold rush—many people hunting for gold in one place

jets—powerful streams of water shooting from a hose

stake—to make a claim to a plot of land for mining

strike it rich—to become rich finding gold